CHOSEN
BUT NAUGHTY
(Revised Edition)

Abraham Obadare

ISBN 979-8-88644-158-1 (Paperback)
ISBN 979-8-88644-159-8 (Digital)

Edited by Funmi Awosiyan and Julius Ogunnaya
Previewed by Abimbola Rotobi

All scripture quotations are from the King James,
New King James, and the New International
Versions of the Bible unless otherwise stated.

Covenant Books
11661 Hwy 707
Murrells Inlet, SC 29576
www.covenantbooks.com

To all people who are seeking a final solution to their recurring problems through Jesus Christ and to those who will also use the knowledge gained in the book to assist others.

CONTENTS

ACKNOWLEDGMENTS

My sincere appreciation goes to the Holy Spirit, who is my guide and teacher, and to my wife and children, who have supported me in this great work.

I also appreciate my parents, Apostle Dr. T. O. and Mrs. E. A. Obadare, who have given me a good direction in the Lord Jesus Christ since my youth.

Many thanks to all the church workers who continuously support me in ministry and those who encourage me to put God's revelations into writing.

PREVIEW

An alternative title perhaps could have been how our decisions can make or break future generations or how to stop tomorrow's afflictions upon your generations. Regardless of your title preference, *Chosen but Naughty* is appropriate. This is not a self-help book. It is tailored to bring awareness to anyone experiencing reoccurring problems (or patterns) existing through generational lines. Any reader searching to understand the reasons behind their problems and seeking possible solutions to those problems will be encouraged by the book titled *Chosen but Naughty*. The reader should not be fooled by the title into believing the theme is encouraging a naughty lifestyle just because you are a child of God! Far from it!

Chosen but Naughty reveals ways in which lives can be negatively affected if care is not taken. The book cites examples of characters from the Bible whose lives began as chosen and celebrated people. They started off as prominent characters in positions of authority but were later influenced by the carelessness of rebellious decisions which, in the end, affected their lives adversely and the lives of their children, bringing the judgment of God against their generation. The author will walk you through the various ways our decisions affect not only us but those around us and into the future. I personally like the section that cautions ministers of God who believe that just because they are working for God, they can neglect their families, and God will grant them special treatment because of their service. The author further reminds the reader to beware of the lust of the eyes, the lust of the flesh, and lusting after things of the world.

This is a must-read for all, and I recommend that the reader heed the warnings of the author and apply the solutions offered in the book. Since we are in perilous times which promote destructive behaviors, *Chosen but Naughty* is timely because it serves as a reminder to the Christian community about the importance of godly living according to the laws of God. Carelessness, rebellion, and unbelief are all acts of disobedience in the eyes of God. The author has clearly depicted them in his book; he cites examples and the consequences of choosing this path. Every decision we make has a cost attached to it, and it is our individual responsibility to ensure its affordability is favorable in our lives and in the lives of others.

Let the reader not despair! For there is hope in any situation the reader may be experiencing. The author makes it clear that it is never too late for God to rebuild your life if you approach him and seek his help. The deepest lesson the book teaches is this—despite our background, the tender care, sufficient provision, and the ever-present help which the Lord extends to his children, whatever level of their Christian journey, are always available to His children. That is if you know what to do and how to do it. Buy the book. It walks you through what steps to take!

Abimbola Rotobi

INTRODUCTION

I congratulate you for picking up this book because the Lord has assigned me to explain some hidden things that will shed light and bring freedom into certain areas of your life. Let me first tell you that God created you for His pleasure and therefore chose you for goodness and His praise. He made you and your children special in His sight, for signs and wonders. He derives pleasure in lifting you up from the pits of hell and various unhappy circumstances. As He does these, He also wants you to fulfill His purpose, that is, continuously live a life of praise and honor to His name, but sometimes we opt for our own designs and desires—influenced by flesh not by His Spirit—rejecting God. This is where the title of this book *Chosen but Naughty* becomes clear.

To be classified as *Chosen but Naughty* is to start off with God and later end up with flesh and evil. This deviation brings a lot of unpleasantness into the lives of people and their generations. Sometimes, chosen people become naughty in the quest for comfort, survival, fame, power, or even because of greed and loss of divine guidance, not considering the consequences. In search of knowledge, Adam, the chosen, became naughty. In search of power, revelation, and victory, the chosen King Saul became naughty—taking laws into his own hands, seeking to kill David, and consulting with a witch. Is there a power, force, spirit, or enticement pressuring you from godliness into disobedience? Do you find yourself leaving the lifestyle of a chosen, highly decorated, and beloved one for a naughty life? The consequences are grave, but God will deliver you in Jesus's name.

These days all over the world, there are so many unpleasant situations in people's lives so much so that they wonder why these situations exist. Everyone is trying to understand the reasons for the various problems and searching for possible solutions. Without any doubt, some of the problems are traceable to what the people before us have done. In this book, I will endeavor to show that your actions today will greatly determine what becomes of your offspring tomorrow and that the actions of your parents and grandparents have a lot to do with what you may be going through today unless there is a divine intervention through the word and the blood of Jesus.

My prayer for you is that the blood of Jesus will flush your lineage and remove every curse. The Lord will destroy every disease or recurring trouble traceable to your lineage as you read this book. Marital, financial, health, career, spiritual, and those various household troubles do not have to continue with you. They will stop now because Jesus will intervene.

CHAPTER 1

Mr. Calos and His Chief Enemy

Blessed is he, whose transgression is forgiven, whose sin is covered.
—Psalm 32:1 (NKJV)

It is customary to pray that God should deliver us from our enemies. This chapter will give an insight into the strongest enemy from which you need deliverance. There are all kinds of enemies, all of which man has the power to overcome, except one—"the chief enemy." As you read on, you will understand what this enemy is and how the devil, through his influence and oppression, uses it to truncate people's lives.

I am reminded of a movie I watched not too long ago. It was about a young man who started out as a talented artist. He was known all over as Mr. Calos (a fictitious name). This young man was so gifted and anointed that when he sang, miracles happened. Whether he was in a church setting or not, something supernatural took place. While singing, the blind's eyes were opened, the lame walked, and the deaf heard. Mr. Calos was so anointed that God used him to cure even the insane. During his performances, many people gave their lives to Jesus, glory be to God. Soon Calos became so popular all over his country that he got invitations to many functions so much so that there was hardly a weekend in which he would not have at least four presentations. The blessing of God was so apparent in his life.

Environmental Enemy

As I continued to watch the life of this man, I was reminded of the parable of the wheat and the tares told by Jesus Christ. The Bible tells us in Matthew 13:24–28 (NKJV):

> Another parable He put forth to them, saying: "The kingdom of heaven is like a man who sowed good seed in his field; but while men slept, his enemy came and sowed tares among the wheat and went his way. But when the grain had sprouted and produced a crop, then the tares also appeared. So, the servants of the owner came and said to him, 'Sir, did you not sow good seed in your field? How then does it have tares?' He said to them, 'An enemy has done this.'"

One day, he was invited to sing at one of his friends' wedding. He purposed in his heart to present a nice surprise gift to the couple. For this gift, he needed the picture of the bride-to-be in order to customize the gift. Mr. Calos contacted an artist who would use the picture to personalize the gift. This forced him to secretly obtain the picture in order to get it to the artist. Unfortunately, the bride-to-be was kidnapped, beaten, and taken for dead by a hooligan who felt betrayed by the lady's father. During the investigation, the police arrested and charged Calos for murder once they found out that he had secretly removed the lady's picture from the family album, not knowing what he had intended to do with it. It was this environmental/circumstantial enemy that began the ruin of the famous Calos. Thank God he was later exonerated, although he had already suffered some setback. From this, we learn that situations around one could constitute enmity in one's life. May God deliver us from all unfavorable circumstantial cases.

Family Enemy

Jesus affirms in the book of Matthew 10:36 (NKJV) that "a man's enemies will be those of his own household." This parable came alive in Mr. Calos's case. He was born to a mother who was involved in witchcraft. He took good care of her, but his mother often detested his achievements. In her demonic realm, a decision was made to have him destroyed and as such he was offered as a sacrifice in their demonic kingdom in order to shorten his goodness and joy. Surely, he continued to experience various terrible ordeals in life.

Both family and environmental enemies continued to afflict Mr. Calos with different troubles and disappointments of all kinds. He began to lose contracts and invitations. He was struck with sicknesses of all sorts. To the glory of God, however, he overcame all these troubles through the power of prayers. No sooner, however, did he get into another attack. He was in the studio one day when he suddenly came down with a severe headache and started to hear voices; hence, he was admitted to a hospital.

Enemy Within

Man's chief enemy is his own character—which I refer to as the "enemy within." This was the only enemy that could destroy the life of Mr. Calos. The enemy within was the one who finally revealed the naughtiness of this young man. All other enemies could not remove him from being chosen by God except this one. When this "enemy within" arose against Mr. Calos, all indications revealed that there is not a more potent enemy on earth. Even the angels of God could not destroy the enemy within. One could overcome all other enemies, but if the enemy within is not destroyed, there is no future for the person. Once you are able to conquer the enemy within (your own character), you can easily overcome all others.

Mr. Calos's enemy within was nothing other than disobedience that led to self-importance. This stemmed from his failure to repent of a sin he committed during his days of fame. One night, at a crusade, he claimed God had given him a message which God did not.

God has since appeared to him to return to the people and tell the truth, but Mr. Calos refused because he felt such a step would damage his reputation. This disobedience hunted him for the rest of his life and eventually prevented him from making heaven. The Bible has already recorded in Proverbs 28:13 (NKJV) that "He who covers his sins will not prosper, but whoever confesses and forsakes them will have mercy." So the enemy against Mr. Calos's prosperity is his refusal to confess the sin of false prophecy.

Mr. Calos was his own enemy. Hidden sins could serve as your own "enemies within." This young man repented of all sins except this one where he gave a false prophecy. The Holy Spirit had told him that the only remedy for this type of sin was to go back and confess. How many times has the Holy Spirit spoken to you about your character, and you have refused to yield? Mr. Calos felt his self-esteem would be at stake if he confessed, but he forgot about God's own dignity. For his refusal to honor God, he was rejected and lost heaven. This is a classic case of "chosen but naughty." Although he performed many miracles in the name of Jesus and thought that God was so close to him, he missed the mark because he harbored disobedience, an enemy within. Remember, your chief enemy is your character. If your character does not give glory to God, you have an enemy within yourself, which no one can ever deliver you from. You are the only one who has the ability to deliver yourself, through confession and repentance. For King Pharaoh it was stubbornness; for King Ahab and the servant of Elisha, Gehazi, it was greed; for Solomon, it was strange women; for Ananias and Saphira, it was the love of money, selfishness, and lying to the Holy Spirit; for Nabal, it was selfishness and lack of remorse or repentance. What's yours?

Please go and study Psalm 32 very well, and the Lord will open your mind to understanding. In this psalm, David proclaimed that the only person who is blessed is the one whose transgression is forgiven and whose sin is covered. He explains that when he was silent about his sins, he only grew sick, lonely, and powerless (verses 3–4). He thought he could cover his own sins, forgetting that God knows everything. He forgot that God is the only one who could decide whether or not to impute sin. He did not realize that the only sin that is truly covered is the one covered by the blood of Jesus.

There Is a Way Out

Honor God above yourself; turn to holiness today, and you will conquer your chief enemy. Confess your sins and repent of them. This is the only weapon that conquers the chief enemy called the "enemy within." Confession is a big slap in the face of sin. Be bold now and do yourself the biggest favor of your life. God has no pleasure in your peril. You started well, and you will finish well in the mighty name of Jesus.

The moment David decided to confess his sins, just as the prodigal son did, he received forgiveness and relief. He immediately found peace and justification (verse 5). (Also see 1 John 1:9 and Romans 5:1.) He then knew and declared that if one person can be forgiven, others too (including you) can be forgiven (verse 6). (Also see 1 Timothy 1:16.)

After receiving forgiveness, David is now able to talk to God (verse 7), and God responds to him (verse 8). Until our spirits become free of deceit, our communications do not reach the throne of mercy. At the end of the psalm (verse 11), David is now able to sing a song of rejoicing. Refusal to confess his sins was David's chief enemy (the enemy within). This enemy within sapped all his vitality. David's way out is your way out; no longer cover your sins, let God cover them for you through the blood of His Son, Jesus Christ—through confession and forsaking. God is faithful to forgive you. Be free in Jesus's name.

Breakthrough Declarations

According to Psalm 89:11, may the Lord beat down my foes before me and plague those who hate me in Jesus's name.

As I confess my sins right now, I receive forgiveness in the mighty name of Jesus.

I search through my heart with the light and spirit of God, and I release myself from all sins, which I have harbored (enemies within).

CHAPTER 2

Their Past, My Present, and Their Future

> You of this generation, consider the word of the LORD.
> —Jeremiah 2:31 (NIV)

If your situations cause you to ask "Why me?" I wish you would examine the following: What are you doing? What have you done? What has your father, mother, or grandparents done that has brought problems to your household or could bring one in the future, even after you might have died? Do you care about what happens to those who come after you, or are you presently living only for yourself? Job 5:2–4 (NIV) says, "Resentment kills a fool, and envy slays the simple. I myself have seen a fool-taking root, but suddenly his house was cursed. His children are far from safety, crushed in court without a defender."

This book reveals the fate of the seeds of chosen and beloved people who later become evildoers in the sight of God. It also offers recourse to avoid God's wrath. By the word *seeds*, I mean one's "offspring," "children," or "lineage." Many chosen people have become naughty in God's sight by living evil lives. When I say "evil" I mean all works, things, habits (lifestyles), and forces that oppose God and His work of righteousness in the world (Romans 7:8–19). As you know, Satan is the source of every evil, and he uses the heart of mankind as his planning field for wickedness. He is the father of all lies and liars. He was the first one who disobeyed God, thereby passing curse upon generations of mankind forever. Jesus says in Mark 7:20–23 (NIV) that "What comes out of a man is what makes him 'unclean.' For from within, out of men's hearts, come evil thoughts, sexual immorality, theft, murder, adultery, greed, malice, deceit, lewdness, envy, slander, arrogance, and folly. All these evils come from inside and make a man 'unclean.'" Also, James 1:13–15 confirms that God does not tempt with evil. We are often tempted by our own desires, which later develop into sin and later yield generational fatality.

I was inspired by the teaching of one evangelist Adewumi, a minister of Christ for Rural Areas Ministries (CRAM) Nigeria, who taught that generational curses are mostly brought about by sins and actions of the head of the family. From this knowledge, various other facts, and experiences of life and God's inspiration, I title this book *Chosen but Naughty* and focus my discussion on what happens to the "Seeds of Evildoers." Awe came upon me when I read Isaiah 14:20–22 which declared, "The seed of evildoers shall never be renowned."

This book raises such questions as follows:

1. What happens to the children of people who were once chosen but later changed to lifestyles that were contrary to God's righteousness?
2. Could the present unpleasantness of your life be a result of a generational issue?
3. Could generations yet unborn also be affected by your past and present?

The answer to all of the above questions is *yes*, the offspring of the chosen but naughty do get adversely affected from generation to generation, but I assure you in the mighty name of Jesus those generational problems will not continue to plague your life in Jesus's name.

Maybe Mom and Dad could not stay married, but you will. Maybe everyone in your family is poverty-stricken, but God will bless you. It is possible that no one ever accepted Jesus in your family, but my God shall save and use you as a point of contact to save others. Light will shine through you in Jesus's name. God will save your marriage. You and the generations after you will be delivered as God uses the precious blood of Jesus Christ to deliver you.

As you read this book, the grace of God will envelop you. Jesus will do the necessary blood work on you in order to cleanse you from all marks of generational problems. He will fix everything which does not glorify God in your bloodline. You will be saved from peril in Jesus's name, and your sins will no longer be remembered (Isaiah 43:25).

CHAPTER 3

Chosen but Naughty

Behold, to obey is better than sacrifice,
and to heed than the fat of rams.
—1 Samuel 15:22 (NKJV)

King Saul was chosen and anointed by God but in the course of his life, naughtiness set in, and he destroyed his generation with jealousy and disobedience. He tore his kingdom with his own hands and was eventually defeated and killed with three of his sons on the same day.

What Did Saul Do Wrong?

Saul started off as a handsome king elected by God for His people. He received the spirit of God and operated thereby. But as he continued his reign, he usurped the priestly functions and was reproved by Samuel. In 1 Samuel 13:9–14, Saul offered a burnt offering that he was not supposed to offer and later gave excuses for his action. For this reason, God tore his kingdom. The NKJV Bible tells us:

Therefore, I felt compelled, and offered a burnt offering. Samuel said to Saul, "You have done foolishly. You have not kept the commandment

9

> of the LORD your God, which He commanded you. For now, the LORD would have established your kingdom over Israel forever. But now your kingdom shall not continue. The LORD has sought for Himself a man after His own heart, and the LORD has commanded him to be commander over His people, because you have not kept what the LORD commanded you.

Unfortunately, this seemingly "no-big-deal" disobedience marked the beginning of Saul's downfall and the deadly effect on his household. No matter how compelled you feel to do something wrong, do not yield; it may carry generational penalties. It was the spirit of impatience that took over the heart of Saul here. He just felt he had to perform the sacrifice quickly and get going to the battlefield. It is possible also that Saul felt he, too, could perform any sacrificial ceremony that a priest could perform. This is where a lot of caution is needed. It is essential not to change God's way of doing things and assume other people's roles, no matter how anointed one is.

In 1 Samuel 15, he disobeyed God's instruction to completely exterminate the Amalekites. Instead of total extermination, he spared some and lied about it. As a result, Samuel foretold the loss of his kingdom. The Bible tells us in 1 Samuel 15:22–23 and 28, "Then Samuel said: 'Has the LORD as great delight in burnt offerings and sacrifices, as in obeying the voice of the LORD? Behold, to obey is better than sacrifice, and to heed than the fat of rams. For rebellion is as the sin of witchcraft, and stubbornness is as iniquity and idolatry. Because you have rejected the word of the LORD, He also has rejected you from being king."

Samuel said to him, "The LORD has torn the kingdom of Israel from you today, and has given it to a neighbor of yours, who is better than you" (NKJV).

When the Bible says "to obey is better than sacrifice," it means God prefers us to do what He requires than to first mess up and then say "sorry." Yes, if we truly repent, He forgives. But He really prefers obedience to apology. A child could continue to do his own will once he knows that all mom and dad will ask is just for him to say "I am sorry." In fact, many of us have taken God for granted. We do what we do and come back to say "sorry."

Please remember that God is a God of justice and righteousness. The same God who says "If your sins were as red as scarlet, they shall be cleansed as snow" is also the One who says to obey is better than sacrifice. To do the right thing is better than apology. Yes, God accepts "sorry," but He also does not leave any sin unpunished. Can you stand the wrath of God? Saul invited the wrath of God upon himself, the kingdom, and his generations by the sin of disobedience. Warning: Watch out and learn from Saul's errors in order to save your future generations.

Jealousy

Jealousy is a sign of naughtiness. Saul allowed jealousy to drive his motives, thereby becoming an archenemy of David, and he attempted several times to kill him. From 1 Samuel chapter 18, where David killed Goliath till the end of Saul's life on earth, Saul devoted his time to seeking David's life at all costs.

Jealousy is driven by insecurity

Loss of confidence in one's God is a sign of naughtiness. It all began when the women of Israel chanted (after David had killed Goliath), "Saul has slain his thousands, and David his ten thousand" (1 Samuel 18:7). The NKJV Bible says in verses 8 and 9 that "then Saul was very angry, and the saying displeased him; and he said, 'They have ascribed to David ten thousands, and to me they have ascribed only thousands. Now what more can he have but the kingdom?' So, Saul eyed David from that day forward."

When you allow other people's comments to drive you into jealousy, you will be digging your own grave. God was so annoyed with Saul for allowing jealousy to work in him that God Himself allowed an evil spirit to come upon him forcefully (1 Samuel 18:10–11). Saul now made up his mind to pin David to the wall with his spear. See also 1 Samuel 19:10–11. According to God, jealousy is one of the evil works of the flesh that prevents one from entering the kingdom of God. Galatians 5:19–21 (NKJV) says, "Now the works of the flesh are evident, which are: adultery, fornication, uncleanness, lewdness, idolatry, sorcery, hatred, contentions, jealousies, outbursts of wrath, selfish ambitions, dissensions, heresies, envy, murders, drunkenness, revelries, and the like; of which I tell you beforehand, just as I also told you in time past, that those who practice such things will not inherit the kingdom of God."

Jealousy is driven by fear

The Bible tells us in 1 Samuel 18:12–15 that "Saul was afraid of David." The fear that somebody is better or will be greater than one apparently leads to jealousy as we read the story of Saul and David. When you allow someone else's success to create fear in you, jealousy will develop. When you allow jealousy to prevail in your mind, the spirit of God will depart from you, and you will be on your own.

Jealousy clouds the mind

When driven by jealousy, one's thought patterns become clouded; one begins to act with rage—making mistakes and doing mischief of all kinds in the highest order. In Saul's case, just because he wanted to destroy David, he started to kill priests and their family members because he thought they were hindrances to achieving his goal. He believed the report of Doeg against Ahimelech and killed him along with eighty-five others. He killed infants and women too.

The Bible in 1 Samuel 22:16–19 records this horrible incident. We realize that it was not David's success that removed Saul from the throne but Saul's spirit of jealousy, which made him take steps against the will of God.

Jealousy breeds divisiveness

When driven by jealousy, one becomes divisive and a plotter of evil. The Bible in 1 Samuel 18:20–25 shows that Saul offered to give his daughter, Michal, to David in marriage, not because of love but in order to ensnare him and set him up for destruction in the hands of the Philistines.

Let us look at some areas of Saul's errors that were considered evil in the sight of God, which did not only destroy him but also cut short the lives of his children and made life miserable for any of his children who survived. In fact, it was not only the three sons who shamefully perished with their father on the same day, but the Bible shows that another two sons (bore to him by his concubine, Rizpah) and five of his grandsons were also delivered into the hands of the Gibeonites to be killed on the same day by hanging (2 Samuel 21:1–9).

God's reaction to Saul's atrocities

The Bible tells us in 1 Chronicle 10:1–6 (NKJV):

> Now the Philistines fought against Israel; and the men of Israel fled from before the Philistines and fell slain on Mount Gilboa. Then the Philistines followed hard after Saul and his sons. And the Philistines killed Jonathan, Abinadab, and Malchishua, Saul's sons. The battle became fierce against Saul. The archers hit him, and the archers wounded him. Then Saul said to his armor bearer, "Draw your sword, and thrust me through with it, lest these uncircumcised men come and abuse me." But his armor bearer would not, for he was greatly afraid. Therefore, Saul took a sword and fell on it. And when his armor bearer saw that Saul was dead, he also fell on his sword and died. So, Saul and his three sons died, and all his house

> died together. So it happened the next day, when
> the Philistines came to strip the slain, that they
> found Saul and his sons fallen on Mount Gilboa.
> And they stripped him and took his head and his
> armor and sent word throughout the land of the
> Philistines to proclaim the news in the temple of
> their idols and among the people. Then they put
> his armor in the temple of their gods and fas-
> tened his head in the temple of Dagon.

What a shameful death! What a pity! For someone who started out well to end up in such a shameful death with his sons; their bodies exposed and burnt—unbelievable! His head was fastened against the wall in his enemies' idol temple for a public show. This is not the way to end a good beginning. Are you getting the point? It is not only the evildoer who gets punished, their children or offspring also never amount to anything great in life if they live at all.

The Bible tells us in 1 Chronicles 10:13–14 (NKJV), "So Saul died for his unfaithfulness which he had committed against the LORD, because he did not keep the word of the LORD, and also because he consulted a medium for guidance. But he did not inquire of the LORD; therefore, He killed him, and turned the kingdom over to David the son of Jesse."

Saul's story shows us that the spirits of disobedience and jealousy are not to be taken lightly. If you notice any of these spirits in your life, please release them to the cross where Jesus died. If you cast these spirits and attitudes upon Jesus, He is more than able and willing to take them away from you.

It is unfortunate that Saul could go as far as wanting to hurt David even though God had already warned that His anointed should not be touched nor should His prophets be harmed. No wonder the Spirit of God left Him, and he had to resort to consulting with witchcraft mediums. With all that Saul did, his lineage could not possibly find favor in the sight of God nor ever make it in life. We realize that the seeds (children and grandchildren) of this disobedient and jealous man (Saul) did not achieve goodness in life.

Remember, the seeds of evildoers amount to nothing; they are never renowned. What are you doing today that may become unfavorable to your generation tomorrow? Are you disobedient to God's instruction for your life? Are your motives driven by jealousy? This is the time to cross-examine yourself. The Bible says in Job 5:2–4 (NIV) that "resentment kills a fool, and envy slays the simple. I myself have seen a fool-taking root, but suddenly his house was cursed. His children are far from safety, crushed in court without a defender."

There Is a Way Out

It is true that the first chosen king, the most handsome and favored man in the land, became naughty and faced rejection from God together with his generation; but there is hope for you. Are you a chosen person but you find yourself disobeying God? The Lord can renew your heart today. He can refocus your mind to live for Him. Do not remain naughty. This is your opportunity for change in order to steer clear of generational problems. Go on your knees and ask for forgiveness. Ask God to allow mercy to prevail over judgment in your life. Stop chasing after other people's lives, and God will sustain your own.

Breakthrough Declaration

- By God's grace, I will no longer allow my position to get into my head. Jesus will help me to wait always for His instructions before taking action.
- Time and tide will not change for evil for me. I have started well and will finish my race well in life by the special grace of God.

CHAPTER 4

His Sons Were Vile
(But He Neglected Restraint)

Because his sons made themselves vile, and he restrained them not.
—1 Samuel 3:13 (NKJV)

There was a man named Eli. Married with two children, he worked all his life as a priest of the Lord. I am not sure what happened to his wife, but the Bible is silent about this, maybe he lived with the children alone. It could also be that God decided to hold the father responsible for the deeds of the children; maybe this is why their mother's story was never told.

In Eli's household, there was no other job than serving God by doing the works of priesthood. Since this was their primary responsibility, their livelihood was gotten from the church. God made sure that they were well provided for by the congregation through various offerings. However, the two sons got greedy and were never satisfied with the portions given to them. Even before their portions were ready or distributed to them, they took all the provisions in God's house without respect for either God or the parishioners.

These two sons of Reverend Eli, Hophni and Phinehas, were not only greedy for material things, but they were also "womanizers." Since they were not just the children of the high priest but also priests themselves, they began to take laws into their own hands, having affairs with various women in the church, believing they were immune to any form of punishment. The wickedness of these two people persisted for so long that people began to complain amongst themselves and also to the high priests. This same complaint got to God who also saw all their atrocities. Unfortunately, however, Eli, at his old age, had no control over these children. There was nothing he said to them that either made any impact or stopped their horrible actions. A few puzzling questions may be raised regarding this family: Was it already too late when Eli started to warn his children against their evil practices? Could we assume that he never created enough time to train them from childhood? Did he ever tell them the importance and delicacy of their positions as priests? Were they seriously warned against sexual immoralities and perversion? Were they not taught the law enough to know the grievous consequences of greed and selfishness? Oh Lord, have mercy!

There may be some basic biblical instructions that you and I have taken for granted, but thanks to God, the Lord is faithful to fulfill all His words. No word comes forth from God in vain. Although the Bible in Proverbs 22:6 (NKJV) says "Train up a child in the way he should go, and when he is old, he will not depart from it," some parents may consider this injunction to be so basic that they do not take it seriously.

I ask again, could Eli have failed to start training his children while they were still young? It is clear that God would not inflict punishment upon anyone just for the sake of doing so. He is the only one who knows the truth of all matters. If He says in 1 Samuel 3:13 that Eli's sons were vile and their father did not restrain them, then we know that the reason for Eli's punishment was the sin of "failure to restrain."

Look, just because of Eli's neglect to strictly discourage his children from corruption, God declared that long life would no longer be in his lineage. Have you ever considered that ordinary failure to train your children in the way of God could result in mishaps and untimely deaths even in generations to come?

Eli was the high priest when the ark of God was in Shiloh. What was his offense? He failed to restrain his children, Hophni and Phinehas, from vileness. The Bible says, "Because his sons made themselves vile, and he restrained them not" (1 Samuel 3:13).

What was his punishment? "And there shall not be an old man in thine house forever" (1 Samuel 2:32). The Bible shows that both Eli and his two sons died on the same day, as we read in 1 Samuel 4:1–18. While both sons died in the war against the Philistines and the ark of God was taken away, the father died of a heart attack when informed of his sons' deaths and the capture of the ark. Ultimately, the doom upon Eli's house came to pass (that he might fulfill the Word of the LORD which He spoke concerning the house of Eli at Shiloh) when Solomon removed Abiathar (the last high priest of Eli's line) from office for his participation in Adonijah's rebellion, and restored the line of Eleazar, in the person of Zadok (1 Kings 2:27). I think it is safe to say that the death of Eli spelled the end of priesthood in Israel. Starting from Samuel, it was the prophets that took over. Dear reader, if you are a priest, should priesthood end with you, or will you train your children to continue your legacy, by the grace of God?

Yes, you may say that Eli was a pious man who served God with all his heart. However, mere laxity in fatherhood spelled doom for his lineage. Those two sons, both priests, were not only greedy, self-centered, and womanizers. They were also power drunk and could not be curtailed. The Bible says:

> Now the sons of Eli were corrupt; they did not know the LORD. And the priests' custom with the people was that when any man offered a sacrifice, the priest's servant would come with a three-pronged flesh hook in his hand while the meat was boiling. Then he would thrust it into the pan, or kettle, or caldron, or pot; and the priest would take for himself all that the flesh hook brought up. So, they did in Shiloh to all the Israelites who came there. Also, before they burned the fat, the priest's servant would come and say to the man who sacrificed, "Give meat for roasting to

the priest, for he will not take boiled meat from
you, but raw." And if the man said to him, "They
should really burn the fat first; then you may take
as much as your heart desires," he would then
answer him, "No, but you must give it now; and
if not, I will take it by force." Therefore, the sin of
the young men was very great before the LORD,
for men abhorred the offering of the LORD."

This last statement "for men abhorred the offering of the Lord"
is scary. To abhor is to hate. This means that the actions of these people turned church members against worship.

This is serious. All leaders must take caution. When people
begin to hate worship because of your attitude in church, the wrath
of God might follow.

The Bible tells us, "Now Eli was very old; and he heard everything his sons did to all Israel, and how they lay with the women
who assembled at the door of the tabernacle of meeting" (1 Samuel
2:12–17 NKJV). God decided to pronounce divine judgment on Eli
because he was not able to discipline these sons.

Looking at the face value of this father-children relationship,
we may conclude based on 1 Samuel 2:22–25 that Eli tried his best.
However, in God's sight, he did not. While human beings look at
the physical, God searches through the heart. God now accused Eli,
together with his children, of scorning His sacrifice and offering. He
was also accused of honoring his sons more than God (verses 28–29).
Hello parents, God is monitoring the heart with which you take His
commands, as far as child-rearing is concerned.

Although the Bible says in Proverb 22:15 (NKJV) that
"Foolishness is bound up in the heart of a child; The rod of correc-
tion will drive it far from him," societies today have made discipline
equal to abuse, thereby preventing parents and teachers from disci-
plining children. With this attitude, society is getting worse by the
day. There are no moral values anymore. Our societies fail to realize
that foolishness will not just go away unless parents and teachers take
decisive steps to train, discipline with love, and lead the children to

Godly manners. If your children are not controlled from the beginning, they will grow out of hand.

Are you a church leader or the head of the household, the boss, or the person in charge? Let's ask ourselves, what could Eli have done. What other steps could he have taken now that his children were already men of age? They were no longer infants or even teenagers. What kind of discipline could he have imposed upon them? If he took the priestly office away from them, would that have signaled his seriousness about piety? Could God have spared him if he took such a step? How did Samuel come out good, even though he grew up in the same house as Eli's sons? What kind of teachings would those sons say they did not receive? May the Lord have mercy and give our children the spirit of obedience. As parents and leaders, may God grant us the wisdom to take steps that please God in the training of our children. It is unfortunate that Eli started his career as a chosen person, but his negligence in training his children in the way of God made him become naughty. Please learn from this.

There Is a Way Out

God will help you. Yes! You will succeed in training your children in Jesus's name. As you grow old, your children and grandchildren will be your glory, not your shame or your killers (Proverbs 17:6). God will help you to successfully face all parental challenges and responsibilities. The spirit of vileness will be replaced with the Holy Spirit in your children. Eli's case resulted in a mess because of child training negligence, but your case will not be so before God. God will reveal His will to you and your children. You will have the ability to do God's will forever. Begin now to tailor your children to obey God. Sing praises with them and continue to tell them of the goodness of God (Psalm 78:1–4). It is not too late.

Breakthrough Declarations

- God will remove all forms of vileness from my children in Jesus's name.
- My children will fear God and not depart from His ways in Jesus's name.
- Upon my tongue lies the power of life and death; I declare life upon my children in Jesus's name. They will enjoy the way of God and never refuse my instructions or ever bring shame to our generation in Jesus's name (Psalm 127:3–5).
- Instead of reproach, my children and I will be for signs and wonders in Jesus's name (Isaiah 8:18).

CHAPTER 5

Too Busy to Train

Train up a child in the way he should go, and
when he is old, he will not depart from it.
—Proverbs 22:6 (NKJV)

The topic says it all; many people are too busy to get directly and intentionally involved in the training of their children. Unfortunately, though, one of the biggest reasons for parental failure in raising godly children is being too busy with what is considered important: jobs, businesses, schoolwork, crusades, ministry works, emails, etc. In fact, those things may be the service of God, but it is part of an excellent service unto God to spend time in training our children in God's way. Do not overwork and forget your children. Do not assume your children will pick up godly manners on their own. Take time to teach them. Let them come to Bible class with you. Allow them to participate in prayer sessions with you. Give them bible-reading assignments to help them get acquainted with the Lord.

Special Immunity

If you are a servant of God in any capacity, Eli's story helps you to see that you cannot afford to take God for granted and assume He will grant special immunity. In fact, your position as His representative requires more care and diligence. Judgment will begin from the house of God. Remember that to whom much is given, from him much is required.

Many children from Christian homes have grown up not really knowing God, and so they live the "everything goes" kind of lifestyle. These lifestyles show neither restraint nor the fear of God. They wear anything, as long as it could be called clothes, whether their bodies are covered or not. They move around with gangs, speak foul language, and others. One cannot differentiate them from the children of those who do not have Christ. Some children have now resorted to occultism or simply living atheistic lives and such. Unfortunately, this is the case largely because parents have neglected restraint while the children were still young. Proverbs 22:6 (NKJV) says, "Train up a child in the way he should go, and when he is old, he will not depart from it." Some parents say, "The kids have their own lives to live." Some see their children get out of order but say, "Kids will always be kids." No! Do not be loose; this is the time for Godly restraint. Just make sure you correct them in love, not in abuse. You are building your future and their future if you train them now. Solomon was careful to warn in Proverbs 1:10 (NKJV) that "My son, if sinners entice you, do not consent." There are some pastors' children and generally children from Christian homes who put up the "I don't care" attitude either because they believe God will give them special treatment because of their "status" or that they can pray and fast their ways out of punishment. But any child who refuses training will perish regardless of the position of his/her parents. God is not a partial God.

Sad to say, many people do not expect so much from pastors' kids these days. If there is any expectation at all, it is a bad one because of Eli's story. But your case does not have to be like that. You can choose to obey God and depart from evil. You can choose to retain the glory of God in your household. You can choose to prove people wrong and live for God. You can set up a pastors' children forum where you pray to God for the anointing and grace to be faithful; where you can help lift up and admonish each other in the ways of God. Let me tell you, there are some pastors' children who live in the fear of God and you can be one of them. There are also pastors who take time out of their busy schedules to be with and train their children in the way of the Lord. You can be such a pastor, minister, or servant of God. Do not say "God will train them for me. He knows I am busy working for Him." No, that's not the instruction in the "manual" that you carry around. The instruction is that you and I are the ones who must train our children. Therefore, it does not make sense to seek the salvation of others while neglecting the salvation of your own household.

For your information, I am not only addressing children of ministers; as long as you regard yourself as a child of God, this admonition is for you too. God will help you regain focus in Jesus's name. He will lead you to set your priorities right. You will no longer be too ministry-involved to train your children. Please be reminded that the total package of your ministerial assignment includes taking time out to train your child(ren).

Too busy to care

I noticed that the husband of the Shunammite in 2 Kings 4:18–37 was too busy to even know that his son was sick to the point of death. He was never home to care for him talk less of training him. He left all the caring to his wife. This is the same mistake a lot of men make nowadays. They do not participate in caring for their children, helping with homework, watching after their welfare, or being the father figure as needed. Can you imagine for a minute if God was never home when we needed Him? May God save us from this evil. In 2 Kings 4:19–20, the child said to his father, "My head, my head" only for the father to send his servants saying, "Carry him to his mother." He did not even follow up with the child to know what became of him. He was too busy with business. His son had already died at home, and he had no clue. What a shame! Many times, our children have needs, and we just say, "Go to your mother." How many fathers am I talking to? How often do you get too busy to care for your own children as if their mother committed a crime for helping to bring them into the world?

When God revealed this message to me, I became so afraid that I started to pray to God that He would help me to avoid carelessness in the training of my own children. Yes, I pastor a flock, and I serve as a district superintendent over various churches, apart from working in the general secretariat of our national organization as a coordinator. Six days a week I am in the church office from a.m. to p.m. doing God's work the best way I know how to, and I spend a good part of Sunday in the church. But I am being challenged by the story of High Priest Eli, and my eyes have been opened to the task of raising my children well. I am praying that God will give me the grace to give adequate time for my own family—showing them the way of God. I am married with children, and the revelation of this book is definitely good for me and all other servants of God who get too busy doing the work of ministry at the expense of their families. Although I put some effort into the training of my children, I still believe that I can do better knowing that there is always a need for improvement. What about you?

There Is a Way Out

By God's grace, my father is also a priest and a prophet of the Most High God. He spent all of his years as an evangelist who traveled all over the world to spread the gospel, but despite his busy schedule, he and my mother succeeded in praying us into the will of God. They imparted the word and fear of God upon our hearts as children. Glory be to God! Today all of us are in the ministry and are walking in the fear of God, by His special grace. This shows that some parents do succeed at pleasing God in child training; so can you. Failure to restrain your children might bring generational problems while a conscientious restraining from vileness will bring generational sanctification.

I pray for you right now that the spirit of negligence will depart from you in Jesus's name. As you take steps and resolve to train your child(ren), you will receive divine support. God will help you to lead your household to serve the Lord. Joshua made up his mind and said in Joshua 24:15 that he and his house will serve the Lord. You can do it! Yes, you can.

Breakthrough Declarations

- Dear God, I am convicted by Your words, and I hereby decide to change my attitude and schedule to accommodate my children in Jesus's name.
- I receive forgiveness for all my training negligence, and I begin to take responsibility for my children's Godly upbringing in Jesus's name.
- I can do all things through Christ; therefore, I claim God's grace to be firm in training my child(ren) in God's way. They will have the knowledge of God and love justice in Jesus's name (Psalm 78:5–8).

CHAPTER 6

John Kept Back from God
(Robbing The Giver)

Every thief shall be expelled. I will send out a curse, says
the Lord and it shall enter the house of the thief.
—Zechariah 5:3–4

Oftentimes, except when the Spirit of God is in absolute control of one's life, one tends to forget where one's blessings come from. I know a man named John who earned his living as a car dealer. He worked for many years but was never able to save enough money or able to do anything tangible in life. Although he attended church regularly, prayed, and tried his best to be nice, he never believed in tithing. He always thought it was impossible for him to give God ten percent of his income, thereby refusing to fulfill the injunction of God in Leviticus 27:32–34 which says tithe belongs to God. He thought ten percent was too much to part with, not knowing that payment of his tithe would have connected him to Abraham's blessings and God's unlimited provisions (Malachi 3:10). He never knew that it is a way of acknowledging God's goodness and faithfulness (Deuteronomy 26:2–6).

Mr. John never understood that God gave his job to him, and God provided the health and strength to work. He never thought God could share from his money. He considered tithing as his church's way of robbing him of his hard-earned money, not knowing that he was the one robbing God. Unfortunately, Mr. John was never able to finish any project he started, and things were always dry for him. Yet he never thought about making changes to obey God's commands regarding giving unto God what belonged to Him. Mr. John's blessings were blown away, and he never amounted to anything. It is sad to note that many people are in the church but continue to suffer financially simply because they have refused to learn how to give to God. Because they refuse to sow, they never reap. When God says "the thief shall be expelled," He is not joking. When He says He will send a curse and it shall enter the house of a thief, God is not joking. If you do not pay your tithe, you are a thief, as far as God is concerned.

Have you ever considered that ordinary failure to pay your tithe can put a curse on you, which might spill over to your future generations? Malachi 3:9 seems to make this clear. The Bible verse says about offense, "For ye have robbed me…in tithe and offering" and about penalty, "Ye are cursed with a curse."

In Malachi 3:7–12, we see that the people are indicted for robbery and sacrilege by defrauding God of that which belongs to Him. This is a most terrible crime of the highest order—to hold back from the maker of heaven and earth who sees and knows all things. This action violates God, and He is asking, "Will a man rob God?" Is it possible for anyone to attempt to loot God's treasury? God has already warned in Isaiah 61:8 that He hates robbery for burnt offering; we must be careful not to rob Him as no one can stand His wrath. I guess a possible reason for holding back is "lack of faith"— not trusting that one can survive on the remaining ninety percent. Well, Numbers 23:19 helps us to know that God is not a man that He should lie. If He says He will bless us and remove devourers, we must trust Him to fulfill these promises. When you give to God what belongs to Him, you are taking a step of faith, and through faith, God is pleased.

When you keep back from God, you end up losing everything. Listen. Each time you purpose in your heart to hold back your tithe and offering, paying part or none of it, you are looting God's treasury and making a fool of Him. Once He has already commanded that you should bring your entire tithe and offering into the storehouse, any step against this is an attempt to contravene His law. But let me ask you, who can stand before God's wrath? Do you not understand that your faithfulness in your giving is an act of obedience and a definite way of storing up for yourself heavenly treasures? What happened to Ananias and Saphira in Acts 5:1–11? Did they not lose both their lives and the treasures they thought they were keeping back from God? Did covetousness and falsehood not bring unexpected and untimely death? They thought it was wise to keep back part of the price, but it ended up being the most fatal decision they ever made. In case you are one of those who keep your church in lack and barrenness by holding back whole or part of your tithe and offering, I pray that you will repent, reconsider your ways, and return to God. You cannot hide from or cheat the giver. God is the one who gives you everything you have; He knows the quality and the quantity of your possessions. Why deceive Him or flout His commandment? Do you not know that a curse that can extend to your generations is already attached to this kind of lawlessness? May the spirit of God speak to you now as you read. Some people choose to pay all their bills first and then take a tithe from the remainder. This is not right. Note that Abraham, whose type of blessing we all covet, did not remove any spoil before giving a tenth to Melchizedek (Genesis 14:18–24). Being a businessman/businesswoman does not give room for carelessness. Calculate your profit and pay the tithe. Your whole profit is your paycheck, whether or not you take everything home or you invest some back into the business.

God reminds the people that their fathers have committed the same crime, and He had visited them with barrenness and cursed their blessings. Now if God says, "You are cursed with the curse," it means that the curse placed on their disobedient fathers will be visited upon the children that are still robbing God. Isaiah 43:27–28 (NKJV) says, "Your first father sinned, and your mediators have transgressed against Me. Therefore, I will profane the princes of the sanctuary; I will give Jacob to the curse, and Israel to reproaches."

God strictly warned the people in Malachi 2:2–3 that "'if you will not hear, and if you will not take it to heart, to give glory to My name,' says the LORD of hosts, 'I will send a curse upon you, and I will curse your blessings. Yes, I have cursed them already because you do not take it to heart.'"

The book of Zechariah 5:3–4 says there is a curse that goes out to the whole earth upon thieves. Anyone who holds back tithing is a thief and this passage says, "Every thief shall be expelled. I will send out a curse, says the Lord and it shall enter the house of the thief." These passages reveal that the generations of people who rob God are in trouble.

There Is a Way Out

The way out is to make up your mind to trust the Lord with your belongings. Acknowledge Him in all your ways and never forget that everything you have is a gift from God. Also acknowledge that it is God who makes one rich without adding sorrow, as stated in Proverbs 10:22. As you make changes, God will prosper you in Jesus's name. I have seen people who have taken this advice and started to pay their tithe. They are not only being blessed financially, but they are also enjoying peace of mind and good health from God. They no longer face the guilt of disobedience, and God continues to shower blessings upon them as promised in Ezekiel 34:26.

Breakthrough Declarations

- Lord, I will trust you with what I have and never withhold from you again (Proverbs 11:24).
- My generation shall not be damned for robbing God.
- I will no longer give you what costs me nothing (2 Samuel 24:24). I receive the grace of cheerful giving in Jesus's name (2 Corinthians 9:7).

CHAPTER 7

When Riches Grow Wings

Riches certainly make themselves wings, they
fly away like an eagle toward heaven.

—Proverbs 23:5

Many people start out well, but when they become entangled with the webs of ambitions, they become naughty, and their generation later pays for their wrongdoing. Some people start with blessings, but along the way, they allow their blessings to grow wings, and the blessings fly away. Once their blessings fly away, there is nothing left for their offspring. Yes, it is Proverbs 23:5 which tells me, "Riches certainly make themselves wings, they fly away like an eagle toward heaven."

Ephraim

Using Ephraim as a case study, he started out well and was the one blessed to be greater than his elder brother (Genesis 48:8–20), but the rebellion, jealousy, wickedness, and disobedience of the leaders of his tribe became the wings upon which the blessings of Ephraim's tribe flew away (Judges 12:1–7). You may ask yourself, "What did the tribe of Ephraim do?" The answer is right in the Bible. Chapters 12 and 13 of the book of Prophet Hosea elaborate on the deeds of the Ephraimites. Hosea 13:6 (NKJV) states that "when they had pasture, they were filled; they were filled and their heart was exalted; therefore, they forgot Me."

In verse 1 of Hosea chapter 13, the Lord accuses them of pride and arrogance—self-exaltation. They also offended through Baal worshiping, and this brought death. Moreover, Ephraim claimed, "Surely, I have become rich, I have found wealth for myself; In all my labors they shall find in me no iniquity that is sin" (Hosea 12:8). But God found the iniquities of pride and idolatry in Ephraim. Their sayings and ways of life made God remember all their sins (Hosea 13:12). God then declared sorrows and dryness upon them. Ephraim started to bully other tribes, putting fear in their hearts and exalting themselves. But God declared that they should be like chaff blown off.

God's wrath against Ephraim reveals that life's journey is a race—once started, it must be completed. Just because Ephraim began with the blessing and favor of God did not mean his tribe maintained those blessings and favors. Sad to say, many people who were well-to-do before have now become dry, poor, and pitiable. What could have happened? Take notice that God looks for mercy and justice. If God provides for you, make sure you remember the poor and avoid pride and arrogance. According to 1 Corinthians 4:7, there is nothing you have that is not a gift from God.

Riches are tools in the hands of mankind, but when one sets eyes upon them, problems arise. Of course, it is all right to seek comfort for oneself and for the children, but one is not to set wealth as the highest goal in life.

The Rich Man

The rich man who forgot God started to utter foolish words, and his life was taken away from him in an instant. He neglected to give glory to God and started to speak as if he made himself rich. Pride came upon him, and he started to speak, leaving God (the Provider) out of his conversation. See the teachings of Christ Jesus in Luke 12:16–21.

Jesus says in verse 15 (NKJV) that we should "take heed and beware of covetousness, for one's life does not consist in the abundance of the things he possesses."

The vastness of property you have will not necessarily lengthen your life; therefore, live a life that gives praise to God with your substance rather than focusing your attention upon your acquisitions. Life does not depend upon possessions but upon the will of God. Do not get too carried away.

There Is a Way Out

Ephraim was chosen to be blessed but became naughty by setting riches as his focus of attention. Let us learn from this mistake and humble ourselves, regardless of the enormity of our wealth. You can be wealthy and still be able to honor God. You can be wealthy and not set your mind on vanity. You can be wealthy and still remember the poor and the less privileged. God is not against your wealth. He himself is the wealthiest on earth and in heaven. He delights in your surplus, but He wants you to set your mind upon Him (the Provider) rather than your wealth (the provision); otherwise, He will blow it away.

Breakthrough Declaration

- From today on, I will no longer set my heart on material things, and pride will not come upon me.
- My generation and the house of God will benefit from my riches in Jesus's name.
- I rebuke the spirit of pride and self-dependence from my life.
- My wealth, I speak to you in Jesus's name that you will not fly away from me. I receive you from God, and there will be no sorrow added to me (Proverb 10:22).

CHAPTER 8

Those Who Make Them Are Like Them

Their sorrows shall be multiplied who hasten after another god.
—Psalm 16:4 (NKJV)

In the mind of mankind, there has always been a craving for visible forms to express religious conceptions. In the Old Testament, people believed they needed to worship Yahweh through one visible image or the other, but God spoke clearly against this. Ultimately, the New Testament states that idolatry includes not only the giving to any creature or human creation the honor or devotion which belonged to God alone but also giving to any human desire a precedence over God's will (1 Corinthians 10:14; Galatians 5:20; Colossians 3:5; 1 Peter 4:3).

People Cannot Rise Above the Object of Their Worship

The Bible says in Psalm 115:4–8 (NKJV):

> Their idols are silver and gold, the work of men's hands. They have mouths, but they do not speak; Eyes they have, but they do not see; They have ears, but they do not hear; Noses they have, but they do not smell; They have hands, but they do not handle; Feet they have, but they do not walk;

Nor do they mutter through their throat. Those who make them are like them; So is everyone who trusts in them.

It is amazing why mankind does things that do not profit or make sense. People put their trust in things that do not talk. People speak to things which they calved with their own hands. This is strange. Have you ever thought about it?

Jeroboam's idolatry brought a curse upon both his sons and the entire nation. In 1 Kings 14:9–11 God says:

> But you have done more evil than all who were before you, for you have gone and made for yourself other gods and molded images to provoke Me to anger and have cast Me behind your bac— therefore behold! I will bring disaster on the house of Jeroboam and will cut off from Jeroboam every male in Israel, bond and free; I will take away the remnant of the house of Jeroboam, as one takes away refuse until it is all gone. The dogs shall eat whoever belongs to Jeroboam and dies in the city, and the birds of the air shall eat whoever dies in the field; for the LORD has spoken!

Also, read 2 Kings 17:21–22.

We later realized that, except for one of his sons who was buried in peace, every other one died as a result of one kind of violence or the other.

The Bible tells us in 1 Kings 14:12–18 (NKJV):

> Arise therefore, go to your own house. When your feet enter the city, the child shall die. And all Israel shall mourn for him and bury him, for he is the only one of Jeroboam who shall come to the grave, because in him there is found something good toward the LORD God of Israel in the house

of Jeroboam. Moreover, the LORD will raise up for Himself a king over Israel who shall cut off the house of Jeroboam; this is the day. What? Even now! For the LORD will strike Israel, as a reed is shaken in the water. He will uproot Israel from this good land, which He gave to their fathers, and will scatter them beyond the river, because they have made their wooden images, provoking the LORD to anger. And He will give Israel up because of the sins of Jeroboam, who sinned and who made Israel sin. Then Jeroboam's wife arose and departed and came to Tirzah. When she came to the threshold of the house, the child died. And they buried him; and all Israel mourned for him, according to the word of the LORD which He spoke through His servant Ahijah the prophet.

Various kings and fathers after him did evil and perished before the nation finally went into captivity. What you are doing today may affect your future generations greatly.

Prayers were taken out of schools yesterday, and violence has become prevalent in them today. The Ten Commandments are being taken out of our public places today. Who knows what will become of justice tomorrow? People are now advocating seriously that Christmas trees should be referred to as holiday trees because the word *Christmas* is imposing Christianity upon them. Who knows what's next? The Bible has made it clear in Galatians 6:7–9 (NKJV), "Do not be deceived, God is not mocked; for whatever a man sows, that he will also reap. For he who sows to his flesh will of the flesh reap corruption, but he who sows to the Spirit will of the Spirit reap everlasting life. And let us not grow weary while doing good, for in due season we shall reap if we do not lose heart."

Please note that idolatry is not limited to bowing down before a graven image. It includes placing anything, in order of importance, to be first before God. It is anything you hold to be more important in your life than God. Your idol is anything you'd rather be doing or paying attention to than serving God either at a particular given time or generally in the course of your life. This could be your job, spouse, money, your socially acceptable ideologies, etc. Psalm 16:4 (NKJV) says, "Their sorrows shall be multiplied who hasten after another god." I would like you to gain wisdom from the words and lamentation of King Solomon in the book of Ecclesiastes. He said all the things we hold so dear in life are meaningless. They amount to vanity. He said he veered off to try some folly and madness but came to realize that all is vanity. Solomon helps us to see that chasing after wealth and various belongings still does not satisfy. Being married to several women or having so many girlfriends/boyfriends neither create nor bring any deep sense of satisfaction. Building mansions and having exotic yards and lucrative farms still amount to vanity. He sobbed in Ecclesiastes 2:18–19, saying that at the end of it all, one has to leave everything behind once death sets in. One leaves them to another person to have; and who knows who will inherit everything I have labored for—whether the inheritor will be a fool or a wise person?

Solomon moved on to give the best advice one could receive in life. He said the conclusion of the matter is that one should "fear God and keep His commandments, for this is the whole duty of man. For God will bring every work into judgment, including every secret thing, whether good or evil" (Ecclesiastes 12:13–14).

Do not allow the pleasures of life, accomplishments, and possessions to become idols in your life. God will not share His glory with anyone. Surrender totally to Jesus now and deposit the treasures of your heart in heaven—the kingdom of the peace of God. If you fear God and leave the same legacy for your children by teaching them the way of God, you and your generations will prosper.

Self-will, self-sufficiency, and conscious disobedience also are forms of idolatry that must be subdued. The Bible passage 1 Samuel 15:23 (NKJV) implies that even arrogance and stubbornness are idolatry. It reads, "For rebellion is as the sin of witchcraft, and stubbornness is as iniquity and idolatry. Because you have rejected the word of the LORD, He also has rejected you from being king."

In Jeremiah 2:1–9 and 13, God said His people have committed the evils of forsaking Him—"the fountain of living water, and hewing themselves cisterns—broken cisterns that can hold no water." This means the people were looking for God everywhere and getting attached to things that replaced God in their hearts. Unfortunately, they were neither able to find God nor detach themselves from wrongdoing since they had gotten enmeshed in those ways of life.

By any chance, do you find any idol in your life that you need to forsake now in order to prevent your next generations from God's wrath? Remember, those who make idols are like them. Idols are an abomination unto the Lord.

There Is a Way Out

Ezekiel 14:6 offers a solution to this problem: just return to Christ, the fountain of life. Repent and turn your face from abomination. I want you to know that God has no pleasure in the death of the wicked. He always hopes that the wicked will come to repentance. God will wash you and make you thrive like a plant in the field. It is not too late for God to turn your life around. Choose to focus on Jesus alone and begin to acknowledge Him in all your ways. I tell you; God will return to you. In 2 Chronicles 7:14–15 (NKJV), God promises, "If My people who are called by My name will humble themselves and pray and seek My face and turn from their wicked ways, then I will hear from heaven, and will forgive their sin and heal their land. Now My eyes will be open and My ears attentive to prayer made in this place."

If you turn, you will prevent your future generations from the destruction that follows idolatry. Do not be like Jeroboam who exposed his household, nation, and lineage to terrible perils.

Breakthrough Declarations

- In Jesus's name, I receive forgiveness for not putting God first in my life.
- Lord, take preeminence in my life and prevent me from putting other things in Your place (Matthew 6:33).
- I reject every form of idolatry and its dominion over my life in Jesus's name. The God of Shadrach, Meshach, and Abednego shall be my God (Daniel 3:7–30).

CHAPTER 9

One-Time Flesh Encounter

And your sons shall be shepherds in the wilderness
forty years and bear the brunt of your infidelity.
—Numbers 14:33–35

David was another God-chosen person who got into naughty activities, which brought terrible punishment upon him and his household. Although he did not directly kill Uriah with his own hands, he directed the murder just to cover up his affair with Uriah's wife. One must realize that when attempts are made to cover up a sin, another sin is usually committed. Because of his affair with Bathsheba and the killing of her husband, God pronounced upon him that the sword would never depart from his household. Although David was a man after God's heart, God's judgment shows that He is not a respecter of persons; hence, David still suffered the consequences, and his household paid dearly for the adultery and murder. His household became a household of wars after wars (2 Samuel 11:2–27). Here is God's judgment upon him:

> Then Nathan said to David, "You are the man! This is what the LORD, the God of Israel, says: 'I anointed you king over Israel, and I delivered you from the hand of Saul. I gave your master's house to you, and your master's wives into your arms. I

gave you the house of Israel and Judah. And if all this had been too little, I would have given you even more. Why did you despise the Word of the LORD by doing what is evil in his eyes? You struck down Uriah the Hittite with the sword and took his wife to be your own. You killed him with the sword of the Ammonites. Now, therefore, the sword will never depart from your house, because you despised me and took the wife of Uriah the Hittite to be your own.' This is what the LORD says: 'Out of your own household I am going to bring calamity upon you. Before your very eyes I will take your wives and give them to one who is close to you, and he will lie with your wives in broad daylight. You did it in secret, but I will do this thing in broad daylight before all Israel'" (2 Samuel 12:7–12 NIV).

No wonder disrespects and various forms of disorders prevailed in his kingdom throughout. In fact, Absalom slept with his father, David's concubines, in public ("in the sight of all Israel" [2 Samuel 16:22])—as fulfillment of the above judgment; and it was in battles that his sons, Amnon (2 Samuel 13:29), Absalom (2 Samuel 18:14), and Adonijah (1 Kings 2:24–25) perished. Oh my God, this is heavy. Although David slept with Bathsheba in the secret, his own concubines were violated in public. Please repent now so that shame will not come upon you.

David's lust influenced his sons Solomon and Amnon. David took eight wives. No wonder Solomon took 700 wives and 300 concubines, who later stole his heart away from God. Although he had been warned in 1 Kings 9:6–9 not to sway from God's commandment, unfortunately, 1 Kings 11:1–13 (NKJV) says:

But King Solomon loved many foreign women, as well as the daughter of Pharaoh: women of the Moabites, Ammonites, Edomites, Sidonians, and

Hittites—from the nations of whom the Lord had said to the children of Israel, "You shall not intermarry with them, nor they with you. Surely, they will turn away your hearts after their gods." Solomon clung to these in love. And he had seven hundred wives, princesses, and three hundred concubines; and his wives turned away his heart. For it was so, when Solomon was old, that his wives turned his heart after other gods; and his heart was not loyal to the Lord his God, as was the heart of his father David. Solomon did evil in the sight of the Lord, and did not fully follow the Lord, as did his father David. Then Solomon built a high place for Chemosh the abomination of Moab, on the hill that is east of Jerusalem, and for Molech the abomination of the people of Ammon. And he did likewise for all his foreign wives, who burned incense and sacrificed to their gods. So the Lord became angry with Solomon because his heart had turned from the Lord God of Israel, who had appeared to him twice and had commanded him concerning this thing, that he should not go after other gods; but he did not keep what the Lord had commanded. Therefore, the Lord said to Solomon, "Because you have done this, and have not kept My covenant and My statutes, which I have commanded you, I will surely tear the kingdom away from you and give it to your servant. Nevertheless, I will not do it in your days, for the sake of your father David; I will tear it out of the hand of your son. However, I will not tear away the whole kingdom; I will give one tribe to your son for the sake of my servant David, and for the sake of Jerusalem which I have chosen."

The flesh encounter could be just once, but it may have a generational consequence. Solomon started well, but his entanglement with many women and gods brought a lasting curse upon his generation. Please be careful, as a man, not to follow every woman your eyes see; and as a woman, not to go with every man you behold.

Amnon, David's first son ended up raping his blood sister, Tamar. The Bible tells us in 2 Samuel 13:1–24 (NKJV):

> After this, Absalom the son of David, had a lovely sister, whose name was Tamar; and Amnon the son of David loved her. He took hold of her and said to her, "Come, lie with me, my sister." And she answered him, "No, my brother, do not force me, for no such thing should be done in Israel. Do not do this disgraceful thing! And I, where could I take my shame? And as for you, you would be like one of the fools in Israel. Now therefore, please speak to the king; for he will not withhold me from you. However, he would not heed her voice; and being stronger than she, he forced her and lay with her. Then Amnon hated her exceedingly, so that the hatred with which he hated her was greater than the love with which he had loved her. And Amnon said to her, "Arise, be gone!"

Incest, womanizing, child abuse, spouse abuse, and drug abuse pattern may easily continue in your generation if you don't ask for forgiveness and repent now. Think about it. What are you doing today that may affect your future generation? Leviticus 26:39 (NKJV) affirms that people waste away because of their fathers' sin, "And those of you who are left shall waste away in their iniquity in your enemies' lands; also in their fathers' iniquities, which are with them, they shall waste away."

Did You Know the Bible Speaks About the Following?

The Bible tells us in Leviticus 18:6–28 (NIV):

> No one is to approach any close relative to have sexual relations. I am the LORD.
>
> Do not dishonor your father by having sexual relations with your mother. She is your mother; do not have relations with her. Do not have sexual relations with your father's wife; that would dishonor your father.
>
> Do not have sexual relations with your sister, either your father's daughter or your mother's daughter, whether she was born in the same home or elsewhere.
>
> Do not have sexual relations with your son's daughter or your daughter's daughter; that would dishonor you.
>
> Do not have sexual relations with the daughter of your father's wife, born to your father; she is your sister.
>
> Do not have sexual relations with your father's sister; she is your father's close relative. Do not have sexual relations with your mother's sister, because she is your mother's close relative. Do not dishonor your father's brother by approaching his wife to have sexual relations; she is your aunt.
>
> Do not have sexual relations with your daughter-in-law. She is your son's wife; do not have relations with her.
>
> Do not have sexual relations with your brother's wife; that would dishonor your brother.

Do not have sexual relations with both a woman and her daughter. Do not have sexual relations with either her son's daughter or her daughter's daughter; they are her close relatives. That is wickedness.

Do not take your wife's sister as a rival wife and have sexual relations with her while your wife is living.

Do not approach a woman to have sexual relations during the uncleanness of her monthly period.

Do not have sexual relations with your neighbor's wife and defile yourself with her.

Do not give any of your children to be sacrificed to Molech, for you must not profane the name of your God. I am the LORD.

Do not lie with a man as one lies with a woman; that is detestable. Do not have sexual relations with an animal and defile yourself with it. A woman must not present herself to an animal to have sexual relations with it; that is a perversion.

Do not defile yourselves in any of these ways, because this is how the nations that I am going to drive out before you became defiled. Even the land was defiled; so, I punished it for its sin, and the land vomited out its inhabitants. But you must keep my decrees and my laws. The native-born and the aliens living among you must not do any of these detestable things, for all these things were done by the people who lived in the land before you, and the land became defiled. And if you defile the land, it will vomit you out as it vomited out the nations that were before you.

These are very serious warnings by God, which everyone must adhere to. Be informed and avoid peril. The more of these detestable things we do, the worst our situations, families, lands, and nations become. Run from such flesh encounters.

Children Suffer Because of Parents' Sins

The Bible tells us in Numbers 14:33–35:

> And your sons shall be shepherds in the wilderness forty years, and bear the brunt of your infidelity, until your carcasses are consumed in the wilderness. According to the number of the days in which you spied out the land, forty days, for each day you shall bear your guilt one year, namely forty years, and you shall know My rejection. I the LORD have spoken this; I will surely do so to all this evil congregation who are gathered together against Me. In this wilderness they shall be consumed, and there they shall die.

Sin came into the world through one man—Adam. Romans 5:12–13 (NKJV) says, "Therefore, just as through one man's sin entered the world, and death through sin, and thus death spread to all men, because all sinned. For until the law, sin was in the world, but sin is not imputed when there is no law." Adam was chosen, but he became naughty when he bowed to disobedience and everyone on earth is now paying for it. What are you doing today that could have an adverse effect on your generations to come?

Hallelujah, there is someone who has laid His life down for you, however. Salvation has now come through this one man—Jesus Christ (Romans 5:15–17). When you accept Jesus Christ as your Lord and Savior, He will make all things new. When you pray to God in Jesus's name, God will heal your life. He will start afresh with you and the sins of your generations will be remembered no more. Are you willing to have God turn things around? He is willing to do it through the name of His Son, Jesus. Luke 1:37 says, "For with God, nothing shall be impossible."

Watch What Comes out of Your Mouth

If you curse your lineage today, it might just come true tomorrow. A curse is a pronunciation, prayer, or utterance to harm or bring misfortune upon someone. Many people are stagnant, unproductive, or experiencing slow progress today because of certain utterances someone in their generation made in their past years. In anger, rage, and desperation, the mob cursed themselves as they pushed to have Jesus crucified at all costs. In Matthew 27:20–25 (NKJV), we read:

> But the chief priests and elders persuaded the multitudes that they should ask for Barabbas and destroy Jesus. The governor answered and said to them, "Which of the two do you want me to release to you?" They said, "Barabbas!" Pilate said to them, "What then shall I do with Jesus who is called Christ?" They all said to him, "Let Him be crucified!" Then the governor said, "Why, what evil has He done?" But they cried out all the more, saying, "Let Him be crucified!" And all the people answered and said, "His blood be on us and on our children.

Who knows what this self-inflicted curse is causing in the lives of innocent generations today? May God have mercy. Please be watchful of your utterances. Whatever comes from your mouth must glorify God. It must be words of peace and blessing. Bless and curse not. As blessings come to pass, so do curses, because the power of life and death is upon your tongue.

There Is a Way Out

You can get a turnaround today. Jesus is able to break all generational curses that are affecting you today. He is also able to forgive your present sins that would have resulted in peril later. Joel 2:13–14 (NKJV) says, "So rend your heart, and not your garments; Return to the LORD your God, For He is gracious and merciful, Slow to anger, and of great kindness; And He relents from doing harm. Who knows if He will turn and relent and leave a blessing behind Him—A grain offering and a drink offering for the LORD your God?" Therefore, if you repent now, the Lord will turn from his wrath. Galatians 3:13 says that Jesus has redeemed us from the curse of sin. May you be released in Jesus's name. What you have just read is not meant to make you feel sorry but to help you get delivered.

Maybe you are an elect of God; maybe you, too, consider yourself chosen (of course you are) but sins have made you naughty and driven you away from the love of Christ. There is still a chance for you. Isaiah 1:18 affirms that if your sins are as red as scarlet, terrible as "unheard of," the blood of Jesus can cleanse you.

Use Ezra's Method

Ezra lamented and fasted for the sins of his people before God. His people got into intermarriages with pagans—against the strict warnings of God, but he did not count himself out as someone who did not participate in the sins. He interceded on behalf of everyone. He humbled himself before God, stretched his arms out toward God, and said:

> And I said: "O my God, I am too ashamed and
> humiliated to lift up my face to You, my God; for
> our iniquities have risen higher than our heads,
> and our guilt has grown up to the heavens. Since
> the days of our fathers to this day we have been
> very guilty, and for our iniquities we, our kings,
> and our priests have been delivered into the hand

of the kings of the lands, to the sword, to captivity, to plunder, and to humiliation, as it is this day" Ezra 9:6–8 (NKJV).

After Ezra's prayer, the people themselves also confessed their sins before God, made amends, and received forgiveness. In Ezra 10:2–3 (NKJV), they said:

> We have trespassed against our God and have taken pagan wives from the peoples of the land; yet now there is hope in Israel in spite of this. Now therefore, let us make a covenant with our God to put away all these wives and those who have been born to them, according to the advice of my master and of those who tremble at the commandment of our God; and let it be done according to the law. Arise, for this matter is your responsibility. We also are with you. Be of good courage and do it.

If you are willing to repent now and lament for the sins of your generations, Jesus is waiting for you now. He will show you mercy and turn things around for you. You, too, might have slept with many men or women (as the case may be) before you finally got married. Maybe your wife or husband has not been enough for you, and you still find yourself sneaking out for satisfaction with someone else's partner. God is about to deliver you. He is about to set you free from the oppression of this terrible sin because there is power in the blood of Jesus. Confess now. Be healed now of every torture that flesh encounters have brought upon you. Be restored now in Jesus's name. Remember that God loves you with compassion.

Breakthrough Declarations

- I confess my sins today and those of my generations before me. God will look down upon me, have mercy, and break the dominion of sin over my flesh.
- I pray that God will break the generational curses that are affecting me today because of the lust of the flesh that my ancestors may have perpetrated.
- The Spirit of God overpowers the lust of the flesh in me in the mighty name of Jesus (Romans 8:1–17).

CHAPTER 10

He Forgot His Calling

And he shall be thy spokesman unto the people:
and he shall be, even he shall be to thee instead of a
mouth, and thou shalt be to him instead of God.

—Exodus 4:16 KJV

Many thanks to God for the life of a minister, Pastor Isaac Abugan, who taught in a leadership summit hosted in my church recently. The spirit of God ministered to me to expose to you some of the relevancies of his teachings in the area of a chosen helper who became naughty in service.

Pastor Isaac said, "Pastors and leaders at large are successful when surrounded with effective and loyal help ministers and ministries." For some reason, however, Aaron forgot the major reason for his calling into Moses's life and ministry; this led to his downfall. God called Aaron to serve Moses. The Bible says:

And the anger of the LORD was kindled against
Moses, and he said, Is not Aaron the Levite thy
brother? I know that he can speak well. And also,
behold, he cometh forth to meet thee: and when
he seek thee, he will be glad in his heart. And
thou shalt speak unto him and put words in his
mouth: and I will be with thy mouth, and with

his mouth, and will teach you what ye shall do.
And he shall be thy spokesman unto the people:
and he shall be, even he shall be to thee instead
of a mouth, and thou shalt be to him instead of
God. Exodus 4:14–16 (KJV).

Pastor Isaac also said, "Your Pastor is your prophet. Your pastor is not your friend; otherwise, you will not benefit from his anointing. God says Moses shall be God unto Aaron. If the ministry of help was not important, God would not have raised Aaron. Many people specialize in the weaknesses of their pastors." Maybe that is why Aaron immediately made other gods for the people, without hesitation, in the absence of his master, Moses. When you are chosen to be in the help ministry as Aaron was, but you decide to please the people around you instead of your master, you have taken the route of naughtiness.

Loyalty

"Disloyal people do not have a future," he said. The Bible reads in Exodus 32:1–6:

And when the people saw that Moses delayed
to come down out of the mount, the people
gathered themselves together unto Aaron and
said unto him, "Up, make us gods, which shall
go before us; for as for this Moses, the man that
brought us up out of the land of Egypt, we wot
not what is become of him." And Aaron said
unto them, "Break off the golden earrings, which
are in the ears of your wives, of your sons, and of
your daughters, and bring them unto me." And
all the people brake off the golden earrings which
were in their ears and brought them unto Aaron.
And he received them at their hand, and fashioned it with a graving tool, after he had made it

> a molten calf: and they said, "These be thy gods,
> O Israel, which brought thee up out of the land
> of Egypt." And when Aaron saw it, he built an
> altar before it; and Aaron made proclamation,
> and said, tomorrow is a feast to the LORD." And
> they rose up early on the morrow, and offered
> burnt offerings, and brought peace offerings; and
> the people sat down to eat and to drink and rose
> up to play.

To whom should one be loyal—the people, committee, or the minister? To whom was Aaron loyal—Moses or the people? To whom are you loyal—your God or your friends? People were talking nonsense about Moses, but Aaron failed to defend his master; he instead helped people to make another God. You must be loyal to the minister you are serving. Aaron should have defended his master, but because he either forgot the reason for his calling or did not understand it, he fell. Do not back off from your leader. Defend him or her when they are not there. Teach the vision of your leader so that you won't expire as Aaron did. Although Aaron was a chosen person, his lack of loyalty to his master and his unreserved willingness to please the people made him become naughty before the Lord.

In Exodus 32:22–25, we now hear Aaron making excuses and not accepting responsibility. In fact, he led the people to use the newly carved gods to worship Jehovah. What a useless cover-up. Do you see yourself working for the pastor or the people?

Note: It is to your own benefit to serve loyally. When you serve, you are making an impact. You will be remembered either for the problem you created or the one you solved.

Scars

Pastor Isaac in his teachings said, "Aaron did not want to get scars" (shame or rejection from popular opinion), which comes upon the faithful and dedicated. He wanted the people to feel good and decided to suggest other gods to them. This is what made this chosen man of God become naughty. He failed to realize that the test of ministry is from the scars one receives, not the stars. This was why Paul said in Galatians 6:17 that "From henceforth let no man trouble me: for I bear in my body the marks of the Lord Jesus."

Apostle Paul listed some of the scars, marks, and ordeals that come with true ministry. He said:

> In everything we do, we show that we are true ministers of God. We patiently endure troubles and hardships and calamities of every kind. We have been beaten, been put in prison, faced angry mobs, worked to exhaustion, endured sleepless nights, and gone without food. We prove ourselves by our purity, our understanding, our patience, our kindness, by the Holy Spirit within us, and by our sincere love. We faithfully preach the truth. God's power is working in us. We use the weapons of righteousness in the right hand for attack and the left hand for defense. We serve God whether people honor us or despise us, whether they slander us or praise us. We are honest, but they call us impostors. We are ignored, even though we are well known. We live close to death, but we are still alive. We have been beaten, but we have not been killed. Our hearts ache, but we always have joy. We are poor, but we give spiritual riches to others 2 Corinthians 6:4–10 (NLT).

Any minister or worker in God's vineyard who does not want to bear the marks (scars) for Christ's sake will be listed as naughty before God; and what happened to Aaron will happen to them. Every leader must realize that there is always a cost attached to leadership: self-sacrifice, loneliness in service, criticism, etc. are but a few.

In 2 Corinthians 11:23–28 (NLT), Paul further stated more ordeals he experiences for the sake of Christ. He said:

> Are they servants of Christ? I know I sound like a madman, but I have served him far more! I have worked harder, been put in prison more often, been whipped times without number, and faced death again and again. Five different times the Jewish leaders gave me thirty-nine lashes. Three times I was beaten with rods. Once I was stoned. Three times I was shipwrecked. Once I spent a whole night and a day adrift at sea. I have traveled on many long journeys. I have faced danger from rivers and from robbers. I have faced danger from my own people, the Jews, as well as from the Gentiles. I have faced danger in the cities, in the deserts, and on the seas. And I have faced danger from men who claim to be believers but are not. I have worked hard and long, enduring many sleepless nights. I have been hungry and thirsty and have often gone without food. I have shivered in the cold, without enough clothing to keep me warm. Then, besides all this, I have the daily burden of my concern for all the churches.

There Is a Way Out

Don't give up when pressured. Be encouraged with the knowledge of the fact that God has given you the privilege to serve Him. Be sure of your calling/assignment and represent your leaders well. Do not get involved in insubordination, and it shall be well with you.

CHAPTER 11

I Want It

Then he said to them, "Watch out! Be on your
guard against all kinds of greed; a man's life does not
consist in the abundance of his possessions."

—Luke 12:15 (NIV)

This topic talks about greed—the desire to have more and more. This is a state of mind whereby one is never satisfied. Whenever a greedy person gains something, he/she begins to long for more. This person continues to desire the property of others, which is in direct contradiction to the tenth commandment in Exodus 20:17 that says one should not covet the house, wife, animals, etc. of one's neighbor.

Greed is the same thing as covetousness, and the Bible names it one of the acts of idolatry (Colossians 3:5). Many people want some things at all costs even when it is not within their reach, but the Bible discourages this and in fact states that such people pierce themselves with sorrows. The Bible says in 1 Timothy 6:10, "For the love of money is a root of all kinds of evil, for which some have strayed from the faith in their greediness and pierced themselves through with many sorrows."

Greed Could Lead to Murder

King Ahab greedily obtained Naboth's vineyard. He connived with his wife, Jezebel, and forcefully took Naboth's land and murdered him for refusing to sell it.

The Bible tells us in 1 Kings 21:13–16 (NKJV):

> And two men, scoundrels, came in and sat before him; and the scoundrels witnessed against him, against Naboth, in the presence of the people, saying, "Naboth has blasphemed God and the king!" Then they took him outside the city and stoned him with stones, so that he died. Then they sent to Jezebel, saying, "Naboth has been stoned and is dead." And it came to pass, when Jezebel heard that Naboth had been stoned and was dead, that Jezebel said to Ahab, "Arise, take possession of the vineyard of Naboth the Jezreelite, which he refused to give you for money; for Naboth is not alive, but dead." So it was, when Ahab heard that Naboth was dead, that Ahab got up and went down to take possession of the vineyard of Naboth the Jezreelite."

But God did not spare Ahab and Jezebel. Ahab's generation was cursed. Every male, whether slave or free, in his household was to be destroyed. His blood and that of his wife's were to be licked up by dogs. The Bible tells us in 1 Kings 21:21–24 (NKJV):

> "Behold, I will bring calamity on you. I will take away your posterity and will cut off from Ahab every male in Israel, both bond and free. I will make your house like the house of Jeroboam the son of Nebat, and like the house of Baasha the son of Ahijah, because of the provocation with which you have provoked Me to anger, and made

Israel sin." And concerning Jezebel, the LORD also spoke, saying, "The dogs shall eat Jezebel by the wall of Jezreel. The dogs shall eat whoever belongs to Ahab and dies in the city, and the birds of the air shall eat whoever dies in the field."

This curse came to pass in 1 Kings 22:37–38 when Ahab was wounded and died in battle. His blood was washed into a pool in Samaria, and dogs licked his blood with their tongues. So also does 2 Kings 9:30–37 record that Jezebel was thrown down the window, and her blood spattered on the wall. Horses trampled her body, and she became food for dogs. The Bible passage 2 Kings 10 records that all of Ahab's seventy sons were killed, and so was the rest of his family when Jehu reigned as king.

Greed Brings Lies and Guilt

As soon as Prophet Elijah condemned the action of Ahab, guilty conscience pricked him, and he started to refer to Elijah as his enemy (1 Kings 21:20). Greed in itself is evil, and once it takes root, the truth will become bitter, and it is hated, just as darkness hates light.

In Gehazi's case, after greed had overtaken him and he has collected the money, clothes, and other goods (which he was not supposed to), he then lied to his master. He told Elisha, "Your servant did not go anywhere" (2 Kings 5:25).

Be Satisfied With What You Have

Greediness is an act that ought not to be named or found amongst Christians (Ephesians 5:3). The book of Hebrews 13:5 instructs us not to allow greed in our conduct and to be satisfied with whatever we have, but Gehazi did the exact opposite. This servant of Elisha was a (trusted) chosen person who had worked diligently for his master, but when he entertained naughtiness (greediness), he brought generational evil upon himself and others. He was not content with what he had, even when a specific instruction was given.

You can read his story in the book of 2 Kings 5:19–25. He followed wealthy Naaman and collected what he had. Unfortunately, it was leprosy that he pursued. He got it all right. He got it abundantly, enough for himself and generations following. Greed brought a curse of leprosy upon him and his descendants forever. You see, what you do today may not affect only you. It may have a lasting effect on your generations to come.

If any of his descendants visited a hospital, doctors will conclude that they have a hereditary disease, but doctors would not know its source. From Gehazi's story, we see that it was a curse (due to greed and disobedience) that brought about the spread of the disease. Doctors are not able to cure this type of disease because the microorganism that developed into this is a curse, not a physically treatable or detectable thing. This is deeply serious.

Some things appear to need medical attention, but they may actually have come about due to something a person in the past had done. Things may happen and doctors may conclude that it is sudden death; yes, it is, but it might have come from a curse stemming from greed and disobedience. Please resist greed. It is anti-God, and it can bring calamity to people and their generations to come.

When you read 2 Samuel 21, you will see a physical manifestation of the trouble (famine) brought upon the people because of a covenant made four hundred years before, which was broken. Joshua had made a covenant with the Gibeonites never to destroy them. But four hundred years later, Israel started to destroy the Gibeonites, and trouble (famine) came upon the Israelites. Of course, they did not know why the famine came, but thank God for David who realized what was happening and made the necessary restitution with the people. Is there a promise you have made that you are now breaking? Is there goodness your parents have left that you are now tampering with? It may have a grievous consequence.

There Is a Way Out

God is a covenant-keeping God. You and I should learn to keep promises. God will help us. Learn to be satisfied with what you have.

Do not pursue after other people's belongings. God has a way of supplying your needs. If you remain content, you will spare your generation from evil. The Bible says, "Contentment is great gain" (1 Timothy 6:6).

Breakthrough Declarations

- Greed will not rule over me in Jesus's name.
- I am forgiven and cleansed of any evil that may have been brought upon me due to some past acts of greediness.

CHAPTER 12

Renewed Bloodline

To God the Judge of all, to the spirits of just men made perfect,
to Jesus the Mediator of the new covenant, and to the blood
of sprinkling that speaks better things than that of Abel.
—Hebrew 12:23–24 (NKJV)

Listening recently to an anointed preacher, Pastor D. Akerele, I learned something about "the pattern in the bloodline." He said everyone should take note of whatever is happening to him or her that may be traceable to one's generation. As you read, please pause and think it through.

What's happening to you now that has always happened to everyone down your generational line? Whenever you notice some strange things happening around you, it's time to plead the blood of Jesus—to deliver you from any possible curse. Your level of education will not prevent the devil from attempting to mess with your joy. It is the blood of Jesus that can rescue you.

Medically speaking, doctors sometimes do blood work on people to find out what is wrong with them. They draw blood and run it through tests to determine the causes of sicknesses. So also should you allow Jesus to run your blood work today and fix whatever is in your bloodline, which does not glorify God. Whatever sin, wickedness, disease, or mishap has been running in your family, it won't continue with you or your children in Jesus's name. Jesus is able and willing to intercept every inherited evil in your life and liberate you today.

The only thing which can remove generational curses is the blood of Jesus. Why? Because Jesus had been made a curse for us. Therefore, once you recognize negative patterns, you must begin to plead the blood of Jesus. As wisdom demands that you be soaked in the blood of Jesus, so does wisdom demand for instance that you investigate to know as much as possible about the background of anyone you want to get married to.

Just to clarify what I am saying, look at some bloodlines here: Abraham begat Isaac and Isaac begat Jacob. The preacher says that Abraham lied about his wife in Genesis 12:11–13. No wonder Isaac (Abraham's son) also lied about his wife in Genesis 26:6–9. They both lied because of beautiful women, the fear of human beings, and the fear of death.

Of course, today, many people also lie about whether or not they are married. People cook up stories just for survival. Oh, may our God have mercy. Now Jacob, the third generation, was also a liar and supplanter who deceived his father and stole his brother's birthright as recorded in Genesis 25:29–34 and 27:18–41.

As this family saga continues, Jacob was also deceived by both his father-in-law and his own children. So we see generations of people who were deceivers. Do you notice that your children lie a lot?

Maybe you also lied to your parents? Who knows, maybe they also frequently lied to their own parents? Please note that as disease could be hereditary, so could habits be contagious. I mean lies can run in the family. Therefore, first ask yourself before reproofing your child. Is he/she doing exactly what you, too, had done before?

Since Isaiah 14:20 has affirmed that the offspring of evildoers never matter in life, Ishmael, Abraham's firstborn, never mattered. Esau, Isaac's firstborn, never mattered. Abraham's wife was initially barren; many of these men also had barren wives. In fact, they all had extra-marital affairs. Many things continued to happen down the line, but they did not think it necessary to stop this kind of evil pattern in their bloodline. In Genesis 4:1–24, we read that Cain was a murderer, and behold, his great-grandson, Lamech, was also a murderer—killing even more than one person. God will touch your life now and transfuse you with the blood of Jesus which will destroy the cursed blood cells in your life.

There Is a Way Out

Let me assure you that there is power in the blood of Jesus. You can invoke this power right now to clear your lineage from every curse. Any family sickness or disease can stop now when it comes to you. The blood of Jesus is thicker than the blood of Cain or Abel. It is by the words of our testimonies and the blood of the Lamb that we secure our victory. I speak to your life in Jesus's name that everything that does not glorify God in your family line will stop its flow right now.

In some families, it is habitual for them to go in and out of jail. I release you right now in Jesus's name. Neither you nor your children will return to jail. Your shackles are broken in Jesus's name. The prison spirit in your family is arrested today in Jesus's name. It may be sickle cell disease that runs in your family, but I speak healing into your bloodstream right now in Jesus's name. I declare divine healing upon you, and you will no longer be a carrier of any disease. Jesus sends His words to you now, and you are healed (Psalm 107:20).

The blood of Jesus stops the flow of heart, kidney, and liver problems and diseases in your family. Cancer of any kind will not be your portion. The fibroid problem you have been carrying for so long is destroyed right now in Jesus's name.

Rejoice, oh ye barren, your child is coming in Jesus's name. You are still going to be a fruitful vine in your husband's house. Your children are still going to surround your table. You will still be called the mother of children. Your children will not get any of these diseases in Jesus's name. My Lord Jesus flies with healing in His wings (Malachi 4:2); He will land in your area and heal you. The trouble will not continue.

Please note that you cannot plead the blood of Jesus if you are not born again. Therefore, I invite you to accept Jesus Christ right now as your Lord and Savior, then you shall be saved, and the blood of Jesus can work on your behalf.

Breakthrough Declaration

I invoke the blood of Jesus to flush my lineage and remove all the things that have been accursed, starting with me.

CHAPTER 13

Final Solution
(Tap into the Power of His Words)

Your word is a lamp to my feet and a light to my path.
—Psalm 119:105 (NKJV)

Ask yourself: What is the noticeable pattern in my life?

Do I need a renewed bloodline? Jesus is ready right now to remove every evil pattern that you have inherited. Revelation 12:11 (NKJV) says, "And they overcame him by the blood of the Lamb and by the word of their testimony, and they did not love their lives to the death."

Is bareness traceable down the line in your family? Do people die young in your bloodline, and you are now afraid for your life? Is there a particular disease in your lineage that you already have or expect it? Do people always divorce in your family? This is not your portion. Do not settle for it.

Fight to stop it before it is transferred to your children. Jesus could intervene today; just accept Him as your personal savior and let go of all evil that is present in your hands. Call on Him to prosper your health and soul. The Bible tells us in 3 John 2 (NKJV), "Beloved, I pray that you may prosper in all things and be in health, just as your soul prospers."

Tap into the power of His *Word*; you will be released. Jesus has redeemed all believers from the curse of the law and all iniquities. The Bible says, "Christ has redeemed us from the curse of the law, having become a curse for us, for it is written, 'Cursed is everyone who hangs on a tree'" Galatians 3:13 (NKJV).

If you already have Jesus, then take authority over lineage problems. You don't have to continue under that suffering. Titus 2:13–14 (NKJV) says, "Looking for the blessed hope and glorious appearing of our great God and Savior Jesus Christ, who gave Himself for us, that He might redeem us from every lawless deed and purify for Himself His own special people, zealous for good works."

Judah slept with his daughter-in-law whom he took for a prostitute. I do not know what business he had soliciting a prostitute to begin with. Look at Genesis chapter 38 to read the details. If the spirit of lust is prevailing over your life, I pray that you be delivered in the mighty name of Jesus. Do not look after prostitutes or any man or woman who is not your spouse. The Bible says, "A bastard shall not enter into the congregation of the Lord; even to his tenth generation shall he not enter into the congregation of the Lord" (Deuteronomy 23:2). It was Judah the son of Jacob who sinned, and no king could come from his generations until the tenth generation when Jesse was born. Jesse was the one who finally produced a king (David) in their generation. Matthew 1:2–6 (NKJV) says, "Abraham begot Isaac, Isaac begot Jacob, and Jacob begot Judah and his brothers. Judah begot Perez and Zerah by Tamar, Perez begot Hezron, and Hezron begot Ram. Ram begot Amminadab, Amminadab begot Nahshon, and Nahshon begot Salmon. Salmon begot Boaz by Rahab, Boaz begot Obed by Ruth, Obed begot Jesse, and Jesse begot David the king."

You should be the one upon whom evil and curse would stop. You should be the one who won't go through the regular divorce trend, generational diseases, and untimely deaths. Pray to Jesus now. It's true that sin came through a person (Adam) but thank God salvation also has come through a person called Jesus Christ. He is on your side. Turn to him now.

You who were hated and forsaken before will now become an eternal excellence and a joy of many generations. "Whereas you have been forsaken and hated, so that no one went through you, I will make you an eternal excellence, a joy of many generations" Isaiah 60:15 (NKJV).

Is everyone always afflicted in your family? Affliction shouldn't be your case. Isaiah 60:14 says, "The sons also of them that afflicted thee shall come bending unto thee; and all they that despised thee shall bow themselves down at the soles of thy feet; and they shall call thee, the city of the Lord." Be angry against all forms of evil continuity in your life today and begin to curse the curse of your life in Jesus's name. You shall be set free.

Use the Nehemiah Method

Nehemiah confessed and lamented the sins of his people. He fasted and prayed before the God of heaven; and to the glory of God, he received mercy on behalf of his people and received the grace and favor of God to rebuild the wall of Jerusalem (Nehemiah 1:4–7). His people also repented (9:2). Today you have the ability to stop tomorrow's afflictions upon your generations. All you need to do now is to stop all evil and ask for the forgiveness of all past sins; yours and those of the generations before you. Your children won't have to suffer. Let those who have ears hear what the Spirit of God tells them now.

About evildoers, Psalm 7:14–16 (NIV) says, "He who is pregnant with evil and conceives trouble gives birth to disillusionment. He who digs a hole and scoops it out falls into the pit he has made. The trouble he causes recoils on himself; his violence comes down on his own head." All the stories in this book show that one does not have to be a rapist or a murderer before being considered an evildoer in the sight of God. All forms of unrighteousness and anti-holiness actions are considered evil. Please amend your ways and ask for the grace to overcome the temptations of this preset perilous age.

There Is a Way Out

Glory hallelujah! I am excited to inform you that God is so merciful and has promised that if a wicked person turns from his or her wickedness and does what is just and right, such a person will be forgiven and receive life by doing so (Ezekiel 33:14–26, 19). Aren't you glad there is still a chance for you, and you do not have to bear the generational sins anymore? Further, the Bible says this about the righteous and the wicked. The difference is clear, and it reads in Psalm 34:12–22 (NKJV):

> Who is the man who desires life, and loves many days, that he may see good? Keep your tongue from evil, and your lips from speaking deceit. Depart from evil and do good; Seek peace and pursue it. The eyes of the LORD are on the righteous, and His ears are open to their cry. The face of the LORD is against those who do evil, to cut off the remembrance of them from the earth. The righteous cry out, and the LORD hears, and delivers them out of all their troubles. The LORD is near to those who have a broken heart and saves such as have a contrite spirit. Many are the afflictions of the righteous, but the LORD delivers him out of them all. He guards all his bones; not one of them is broken. Evil shall slay the wicked, and those who hate the righteous shall be condemned. The LORD redeems the soul of His servants, and none of those who trust in Him shall be condemned.

I strongly recommend that you read Ephesians 4:27–32. God's exhortation is that we let go of our old ways of life and walk in newness. Paul, in this passage, says, "Let him that stole steal no more." This is the best way to resist the devil. Resist evil today because your generation is at stake. May God help you and show mercy.

Breakthrough Declarations

- I receive faith to trust what God's words have settled concerning me.
- I receive a word, by faith, which removes curses from my generation. From this moment on, there is no curse, divination, or sorcery against me that will stand in Jesus's name.
- I accept the forgiveness God has offered to me through the blood of Jesus, and I am set free from all guilt.

CHAPTER 14

God Will Rebuild Your Ruin

Thus says the Lord GOD: On the day that I cleanse
you from all your iniquities, I will also enable you to
dwell in the cities, and the ruins shall be rebuilt.
—Ezekiel 36:33 (NKJV)

If You Are the Cause of the Ruin

It is the pleasure of God to rebuild your ruins, but I'd first like you to know that rebuilding takes a process. This process involves humbling yourself before God as a sinner, seeking His face in prayer (2 Chronicles 7:13–15), and turning from sinful ways.

If the source of the ruin is from others in your generation, it is the same process as above. Just know that anything that does not glorify God is not your portion. Then rise up and seek the face of God, pleading the blood of Jesus. The curse shall be broken. Ask God to honor His name in your life. You must realize your position in God. You must know that you are entitled to freedom in Christ Jesus. This knowledge will help you to expect your rebuilding.

Philippians 2:10 says every knee shall bow at the mention of the name of Jesus Christ, and every tongue (whether on earth, beneath the earth, or in heaven) shall confess that Jesus is Lord, to the glory of God. Also, the Bible affirms that the name of Jesus is a strong tower, the righteous run into it, and they are saved. Although you may have been initiated into and shackled by all kinds of unholy and ungodly inheritance, the Lord is releasing you right now in the mighty name of Jesus. Enough is enough! In the name of Jesus, your ruins shall be rebuilt. You shall rise again. You will no longer be followed by curses and dryness. Blessing is about to rain upon you in Jesus's name.

Jesus Became a Curse to Remove Your Curse

Galatians 3:13–14 (NKJV) says, "Christ has redeemed us from the curse of the law, having become a curse for us, for it is written, 'Cursed is everyone who hangs on a tree,' that the blessing of Abraham might come upon the Gentiles in Christ Jesus, that we might receive the promise of the Spirit through faith." By faith in Jesus, I declare that you begin to enjoy the blessings of Abraham. You are no longer inheriting curse, evil, punishment, or stagnancy. I set you free from all bondages inherited from evil generational sins in Jesus's name. Jesus has redeemed you from the curse of the law. No curse, divination, or sorcery against you will ever prosper again. I declare you free from all past demonic lineage in the name of Jesus Christ.

I put you deep into the blood of Jesus Christ and declare you free. Your shackles are gone. Your spirit is free. The Lord lifts you up. Even though the people before you may have perpetrated evil through disobedience and invited curse upon your lineage, the blood of Jesus set you free today. We overcome the devil by the blood of the Lamb. Now there is therefore no condemnation for you because of the intervention of Jesus Christ in your life. Walk free as a child of God. The Bible says there is no weapon fashioned against you that will prosper. I want you to start believing these declarations of God upon your life right now.

God Has Made Up His Mind

Numbers 23:19 (NKJV) says, "God is not a man, that He should lie, nor a son of man, that He should repent. Has He said, and will He not do? Or has He spoken, and will He not make it good?" God has made up His mind to save you from all your old ways, influences, powers, and strongholds. Oh yes! Your ways are about to be made plain. Your old ruins are about to be rebuilt. Once God has purposed it, no one can prevent it, except you (yourself)—if you do not exercise faith in God's Words for your life. Whenever doubt sets into your life, you negate God's promises. See Hebrew 3 from verse 7.

God Will Have Concern for You

Yes, your vileness or that of your generation might have brought God's anger upon your life, but you are being delivered right now in Jesus's name. God says He is going to have mercy on you for His holy name's sake. He will sanctify His great name and have mercy on you. He will terminate your covenant (known or unknown) with all past problems right now. You may have suffered emotional, biological, marital, financial, or spiritual problems, but God is having concerns for you right now. You are being set free. In the name of Jesus, go and be downcast no more.

You Are Being Forgiven

Rebuilding often gets hindered by sin and disobedience. I therefore encourage you to forsake sins and turn to holiness. There is power in the blood of Jesus. Hebrews 12:23–24 (NKJV) declares, "To God the Judge of all, to the spirits of just men made perfect, to Jesus the Mediator of the new covenant, and to the blood of sprinkling that speaks better things than that of Abel." Yes, the blood of Jesus speaks better things than the blood of Abel. This blood was shed for you on Calvary. Therefore, by the words of your testimony that Jesus is your Lord and Savior, and by the blood of the Lamb, I declare you an overcomer right now in Jesus's name.

New Spirit, Blessings, and Rebuilding

God affirms in Ezekiel 36:25–38 that He will clean you from all filthiness, give you a new heart, put His spirit in you, and make you dwell safely in this land that He has given you. He goes further to assure you that He will be your God, deliver you from all unrighteousness, and prevent famine from coming upon you. God will remove reproach from you and lead you to hate your past sins. He says He will help rebuild your ruins. I think you are getting the message. God is going to remove desolation from your portion, and from now on, the powers and influences of the wicked will no longer rest upon your portion. You will no longer be led into temptations. Receive your freedom right now in Jesus's name. The mouth of the Lord has spoken it. In the book of Jeremiah 31:28 (NKJV), the Lord says, "And it shall come to pass, that as I have watched over them to pluck up, to break down, to throw down, to destroy, and to afflict, so I will watch over them to build and to plant, says the LORD."

You have started well; you will finish well. Naughtiness will not destroy you. Your good lot will not be changed to bad in Jesus's name. I say again, may you end your race well. Enjoy your new life of peace in Jesus Christ. You have been chosen; please do not become naughty.

God will help you in Jesus's name.

SOME BOOKS WRITTEN BY PASTOR DR. ABRAHAM OBADARE

Help!
(Men in Trouble, Women in Search)

This book offers help to all people, young and old, single and married. In the book, you will discover ways of keeping out of trouble and maintaining a good relationship God's way. The authors have loaded this book with Godly solutions to whatever you may be facing as far as relationship is concerned, whether your relationship has either derailed or at the verge of collapsing."

Help! is cowritten by Pastors Justus Orori and Abraham Obadare.

My Notebook for the WORD

This journal is prepared with you in mind, knowing that most serious and committed Christians like you have the discipline of writing down all revelations given by God when reading the Bible, listening to sermons and teachings, and others When you take notes, you are able to save and review records for future use.

Enjoy!

Contact (516) 860–5729 for your copy.

LOOK OUT FOR UPCOMING NEW BOOKS BY PASTOR ABRAHAM OBADARE

No Contest When the Wheel Turns

Are you in some situations that you cannot write home about? You will receive comfort as you read this book, realizing that God is able to change your time and tide around. You will drool on yourself in awe of His might as He repositions you into greatness (Ecclesiastes 10:7).

Praying for My Pastor

Do I need to pray for my pastor? After all, he is already very close to God. This book will help you answer this very important question.

The Panel Beater

God panel beat a world that is void, shapeless, and formless into beautiful creations. Any shapeless in your life, God will beat into shape (Genesis 1:1–4).

Marriage Needs

For the married, this book discusses various issues in marriage and shows how to season your marriage with godly sustaining elements.

For the singles, there is enough information here to help you find that ideal man or lady and learn the intricacies of marriage planning until and after you say "I do."

Pastor's Portfolio

How do I manage people? How do I combine my ministerial duties with family leadership? Read this book, and God will minister to your needs.

ABOUT THE AUTHOR

Pastor Dr. Abraham Obadare is the district superintendent of all the Christ Apostolic Church WOSEM branches in the states of New York, New Jersey, Pennsylvania, Connecticut, and Rhode Island in the United States of America and Canada. Graduating from Hunter College of the City University of New York, he holds a bachelor's degree in economics. Dr. Obadare later obtained both his master of divinity and doctor of ministry degrees at New York Theological Seminary, New York.

Pastor Abraham served as an adjunct instructor at Nyack College, teaching biblical interpretation, ethics, managing cultural diversity, faith and worldviews, and many more. He has been serving as a pastor of Christ Apostolic Church WOSEM for many years. This dynamic man of God is also a television evangelist, a newspaper columnist, and a radio preacher.

His ministry is based in Queens, New York. This minister is an effective teacher of the Word of God with a rich experience in church planting and evangelism. He coauthored his first book titled Help!